Main

VOICES FROM PRISON

VOICES FROM PRISON
The Cuban Five

PATHFINDER
New York   London   Montreal   Sydney

Edited by Mary-Alice Waters

Copyright © 2014 by Pathfinder Press

ISBN 978-1-60488-058-8
Library of Congress Control Number 2014930018
Manufactured in Canada

COVER DESIGN: Eva Braiman
COVER IMAGE: *One day my prison shirt will be left hanging there,*
pastel by Antonio Guerrero.

Pathfinder
www.pathfinderpress.com
E-mail: pathfinder@pathfinderpress.com

Contents

Preface

*"When the history of humanity is written, there will
have to be a page for the five Cuban heroes.
They're internationalist heroes, world heroes."*

JOSÉ LUIS PALACIO
Havana, February 2013

JOSÉ LUIS PALACIO'S WORDS give voice to the verdict of millions in Cuba and around the world who are fighting for the
freedom of Gerardo Hernández, Ramón Labañino, Antonio
Guerrero, Fernando González, and René González—known
internationally as the Cuban Five.

Palacio, today a refrigeration systems mechanic in Pinar
del Río, was one of the young Cuban volunteers who fought
as part of the scouting platoon led by Lieutenant Gerardo
Hernández Nordelo in the north Angolan province of
Cabinda a quarter century ago. The platoon was engaged in
mop-up operations following the 1988 defeat of the military
forces of the white-supremacist regime of South Africa at the
battle of Cuito Cuanavale in southern Angola.

In 1991 Nelson Mandela told the people of Cuba and the
world, the "crushing defeat of the racist army at Cuito Cuanavale," won by the combined forces of Cuba's internationalist
volunteers and Angolan and Namibian troops, all under Cuban
command, not only "broke the myth of the invincibility of the
white oppressors." It was "a turning point in the struggle to free
the continent and our country from the scourge of apartheid!"

Three of the Cuban Five—René González and Fernando González, as well as Gerardo Hernández—were among the more than 425,000 Cuban volunteers who made that victory possible.

Today, Gerardo Hernández is incarcerated in the Victorville, California, maximum-security penitentiary. Framed up on charges of conspiracy to engage in espionage and conspiracy to commit murder, he is serving two concurrent sentences of life without parole.

Hernández, Ramón Labañino, Antonio Guerrero, and Fernando González have now spent more than fifteen years in US federal prisons. René González, who served his entire sentence—fourteen and a half years in US custody—returned to Cuba in May 2013. His tireless efforts since then have brought renewed energy to the worldwide fight to win freedom for the Five.

The 1998 arrest and frame-up of the Cuban Five; their trial in Miami, Florida, and summary conviction on all counts, despite overwhelming evidence to the contrary; the exorbitant sentences they were given; the vindictive punishments and inhuman conditions they have faced, especially during the first year and a half of pretrial detention; the respect they have won from fellow inmates for their principled conduct, and the helping hand they have extended to others—all touch a deep chord with millions of working people in the United States. Because millions themselves have had similar experiences with the system of capitalist "justice," or know of the ordeals faced by family members, friends, and fellow workers.

With more than 2.2 million men and women behind bars today, the United States has the highest incarceration rate of any country in the world. Moreover, according to the US Supreme Court itself, 97 percent of those held in federal prisons have never gone to trial. Instead—threatened with life in prison or worse if they insist on their innocence and their right to the trial guaranteed by the US Constitution—they have been blackmailed into copping a plea to crimes they never committed. That each of the Five refused to even consider such a course has gained them enormous respect among fellow prisoners.

The fifteen-year battle waged by the Cuban Five to win their freedom, and most importantly *who they are,* come to life in the accounts that follow.

This is a companion volume to the graphic eloquence of Antonio Guerrero's fifteen watercolor paintings for fifteen years, *I Will Die the Way I've Lived.* It builds on two other titles—*The Cuban Five: Who They Are; Why They Were Framed; Why They Should Be Free,* and *Cuba and Angola: Fighting for Africa's Freedom and Our Own.*

■

The interviews, articles, poems, paintings, photographs, and speeches in the pages of *Voices from Prison: The Cuban Five* have one thing in common. Through them we come to know the revolutionary integrity, resilience, stature, and humanity of each of the Cuban Five. We're offered a revealing insight into their lives these last fifteen years as revolutionary fighters within a large segment of the working class in the United States—those behind bars.

Who the Five are emerges in sharp relief.

Some of the words published here are tributes by fellow inmates whose lives were transformed by friendship with one or another of the Five during their time together in prison.

Some are articles, poems, and messages written by one or another of the Cuban Five themselves. Some are interviews with them, spreading the truth about their prison experiences the world over.

An interview with Elizabeth Palmeiro, who is married to Ramón Labañino, takes us inside the lives of the families of the Five and the ways in which prison officials routinely use visiting privileges as a weapon to try to break both prisoners and their loved ones. And, more important, not only how the authorities have failed to accomplish this but how the Five and their families have fought back.

■

Three *Voices* here deserve to be singled out. They are by or about others who have themselves known many years of imprisonment for their actions in defense of the sovereignty and independence of their own people.

Nelson Mandela, leader of the decades-long revolutionary struggle that brought down the white supremacist regime of South Africa, and the first popularly elected president of that country, served more than twenty-seven years in the prisons of apartheid between 1962 and 1990, many of them under conditions of hard labor.

Mandela's example of resistance and strength has been a lodestar for Gerardo Hernández. He managed to keep with him a photo of Mandela throughout the many months of pretrial isolation in the punishment cells of the Miami Federal Detention Center. His salute to Nelson Mandela reproduced here was written upon learning of the South African leader's death on December 5, 2013, and phoned out to friends during a brief window of opportunity between two extended lockdowns at the Victorville penitentiary.

"The Cuban Five will continue facing every day our unjust imprisonment, until the end, inspired by his example of unwavering loyalty and resistance." No more deeply felt tribute—no more deserving tribute— could be paid to Nelson Mandela.

■

Two other *Voices* are those of fighters for the independence of Puerto Rico who, like the Five, have known decades in the prisons of Puerto Rico's colonial master. Carlos Alberto Torres, released after thirty years in US prisons, pays tribute to the Fernando González he came to know and deeply respect during the five years they shared at the federal prison in Oxford, Wisconsin.

And Rafael Cancel Miranda, who likewise spent twenty-seven and a half years in Washington's prisons for his pro-independence actions, closes these pages with the most profound revolutionary truth for the toiling mass of humanity worldwide:

"Why do we fight for the Five? Because we are fighting for ourselves. We're not doing them a favor. We're doing ourselves a favor. We are fighting for our own freedom."

Mary-Alice Waters
January 2014

Who Are the Cuban Five

GERARDO HERNÁNDEZ, Ramón Labañino, Antonio Guerrero, Fernando González, and René González are known to millions worldwide as the Cuban Five. In 1998, they were living and working in southern Florida when each of them was arrested by US federal police in coordinated predawn raids.

What were their allegedly criminal activities?

They were gathering information on the plans and actions of counterrevolutionary Cuban American organizations, including murderous paramilitary outfits that operate with impunity on US soil. These groups and the individuals who belong to them have a more than half-century-long record of carrying out bombings, assassinations, and other assaults on Cubans and other supporters of the Cuban Revolution—within the United States, Puerto Rico, Venezuela, Panama, and elsewhere, as well as in Cuba.

Since 1959, nearly 3,500 men, women, and children in Cuba have been killed in such attacks, most originating from the United States. The task of the Five was to keep the Cuban government informed of deadly operations being prepared in order to prevent as many as possible from coming to fruition.

The Five were brought to trial and convicted by a federal court in Miami on frame-up charges that included conspiracy to commit espionage and, in the case of Gerardo Hernández, conspiracy to commit murder. The latter charge, added on months after his arrest, was based on the allegation that Hernández had advance knowledge of the Cuban government's February 1996 shootdown over Cuban waters of two planes whose Miami-based sponsors had rebuffed Havana's repeated warnings to cease recurring provocations within Cuban airspace.

Each of the Five proudly acknowledged before the court and to the world that they were working for the Cuban government to prevent future murderous acts from taking place—and they would gladly do so again if asked. On their unbowed heads, the judge imposed maximum sentences, ranging from fifteen years for René González, to life without parole for Guerrero and Labañino, and a double life sentence for Hernández, who led the effort.

Conceding the blatantly prejudiced atmosphere surrounding the trial, a three-judge federal appeals court panel unanimously overturned the convictions in 2005. Following a government appeal, the full court reinstated the convictions a year later.

A 2008 federal court decision ruled that the sentences imposed on three of the five—Guerrero, Labañino, and Fernando González—exceeded federal guidelines. Labañino's time was reduced from life without parole to thirty years, Guerrero's from life without parole to twenty-one years and ten months. Fernando González's sentence was shortened only slightly, from nineteen years to seventeen years and nine months. The court refused even to consider reducing Hernández's sentence on the grounds that he is serving not one but two life terms, so it would make no difference!

In May 2013 René González, after completing every day of his sentence—more than fourteen and a half years in US custody—became the first of the Five to return to Cuba. Also having served his entire sentence, Fernando González is scheduled for release on February 27, 2014. Were they to serve their full time, Guerrero would not be released until September 2017, and Labañino in October 2024.

For Hernández there is no release date. Moreover, as an additional, intensely cruel punishment throughout his entire imprisonment, Washington has denied his wife, Adriana Pérez, a visa to enter the United States to visit him.

The 2009 sentence reductions, however, registered the pressure on the US from growing international condemnation of the trial and the unconscionable length of the prison terms imposed on the Cuban Five. At the court hearing where Guerrero was resentenced, federal prosecutors acknowledged they were seeking to "quiet the waters of contentiousness" and "noise" swirling around the case worldwide.

Since then, moreover, evidence has come to light that a number of journalists writing about the trial in the Miami press were simultaneously receiving payments from the US government's Office of Cuban Broadcasting. This further proof of the corruption of the trial process has become part of the habeas corpus appeals filed on behalf of Hernández, Labañino, and Guerrero.

Why are the Cuban Five in prison for even a day?

Because they are exemplary sons of the Cuban Revolution, of the men and women who brought into being and defend "the first free territory of the Americas." They are held hostage not only as punishment for the audacity of the Cuban toilers who dared to defend Angola's sovereignty, to help free Namibia, and to fight and die to liberate Africa from the scourge of apartheid. They are being punished for the determination of Cuba's workers and farmers to make and defend a socialist revolution in what was once a virtual US colonial protectorate. They are in prison because they represent the men and women of Cuba who to this day refuse to submit to the dictates of Washington.

It was for these deeds the Five were arrested, framed up, and locked away through three US administrations of William Clinton, George W. Bush, and Barack Obama.

The unbending integrity, dignity, courage, truthfulness—and humor—of each of the Five, and growing knowledge of the consistency of their revolutionary conduct from Cuba and Angola to US prison cells, is winning them ever-increasing support.

As long as even one of them remains behind bars, however, none of us is "free."

M-A W

Friendship with René changed my life

RODOLFO RODRÍGUEZ

Rodolfo "Roddy" Rodríguez served time alongside René González in the Federal Correctional Institute in Marianna, Florida. He was interviewed June 13, 2012, on Edmundo García's popular call-in program *La tarde se mueve* (Afternoon on the move) broadcast on Radio Progreso, a Spanish-language station in Miami. The translation is by the *Militant*.

■

EDMUNDO GARCÍA: Today's program is one we've been looking forward to all week. My guest is Rodolfo Rodríguez. He's fifty-five years old and everyone calls him Roddy.

Roddy, you came to the US from Mariel.

RODOLFO RODRÍGUEZ: That's right. My odyssey in the United States began in 1980.*

---

* Rodríguez was among the 128,000 Cubans who came to the United States in April 1980 as part of what was popularly known as the Mariel boatlift. At that time, the US government was stepping up aggressive actions throughout the Caribbean and Central America in response to the 1979 revolutionary victories in Nicaragua and Grenada and sharpening class battles in El Salvador, Guatemala, and elsewhere in the region. Part of the political propaganda campaign orchestrated by the administration of US presi-

GARCÍA: Roddy was in the same prison with the Cuban antiterrorist fighter and Hero of the Republic of Cuba, René González. For several years, between 2004 and René's release in September 2011, Roddy got to know René, and this left an imprint on his life.

How did you meet René?

RODRÍGUEZ: I arrived at the Marianna prison in 2002. In 2004 a hurricane destroyed the place and the National Guard took us out. After two months, I was part of the first group that went back. The next day a group was brought in from another prison, and René González was among them.

I was introduced to him by a fellow Cuban who said, "Hey, man, let me introduce you to the spy." Everyone there called them "spies"—that's the way it was and they accepted that. It's what they were accused of, even though they were never involved in espionage.

That's how I met René, and I can truly tell you it has been one of the friendships that changed my life the most.

I was raised in a home where there was a lot of hostility toward the government of our country. Today I thank God that my thinking is completely different.

I believe in God, and in prison I was seen as the one who brought in religion. I have to tell you that so you'll understand what follows.

When I first met René, right off the bat I told him that I be-

---

dent James Carter was the claim that Havana prevented Cubans who wanted to leave the country from going. The revolutionary government called Washington's bluff, opening the port of Mariel to private boats coming from the United States to pick up anyone who wanted to emigrate. More than 100,000 did before the US government, in an about-face, demanded the Cuban government stop the exodus.

lieve in God. I expected René to take me on, to start arguing with me.

What happened? He replied, "That's great. I don't. But I believe that a true Christian will want the best for humanity, and if my friendship with you helps you become a better Christian, I'll be very happy." That had a tremendous impact on me.

So that's how our friendship began. We lived two cells apart. We weren't cellmates because we each had too many things—especially books—to fit in the same cell. We would see each other whenever the doors were opened, except when René went running. It wasn't easy to keep up with him—he ran a lot.

It was my relationship with René that began changing the way I thought. I began to see things for myself, and eventually I was convinced.

In prison I met people from different countries—out of respect, I don't want to mention which ones—and it pained me to notice that some couldn't read or write. Then I thought about the Cuban people—even those who are here—and I told myself, "Wow, there's not a single one who doesn't know how to read! I come from a country that's been blessed."

Now I understand all the positive sides of Cuba that I didn't see before. And all that I began to understand thanks to René.

René is a man of principles, like all of the Five. He would tell me, "Principles have no price, because whoever has them won't sell them, and whoever sells himself doesn't have principles." I believe their principles have helped make them popular and respected in the prisons they've been in.

I'll never forget the time René got me a book of Bible stories from the library. He asked me, "Would you like to read this book together?" It was in English—I can read English but he reads it well—and he began to translate it into Spanish. We read the whole book—the story of Abraham, everything.

Things like that made me realize René was not some fanatic, that he was true to his principles. He lives up to what he says. You can tell him what you think, without upsetting him. He respects your ideas. "You have the right to say what you think," he'd always say. "Just as I have the right to think as I do."

GARCÍA: Did other prisoners have the same respect for him?

RODRÍGUEZ: I think everyone did. I'll never forget this young Black guy, his cellmate, who composed a rap song with a political theme about the US and sang it for everyone in the yard where we held events on special occasions like July 4 or Christmas Eve. I can't tell you exactly what his political ideas were, but I think perhaps he was inspired by his relationship with René, by coming to understand the cause of the Five. Many people didn't know what was happening around the Five and when they learned they were surprised. We even had a T-shirt made with the symbol of the Five and the star from the Cuban flag.

GARCÍA: What did you do on a typical day in those years?

RODRÍGUEZ: René ran a lot, as I said. And when he wasn't running he was reading. You could see the solidarity he got from around the world by the mail he received. It was a moment we all looked forward to every day—seeing tons of letters come in, and all to one address, René's: from Australia, Russia, China, from all over. Some inmates would say to him, "Listen, save me the stamps." In fact, I have a lot of them myself.

He would get a lot of letters from Cuba—from people in the churches, even from prison inmates. At a prison in Granma province, some inmates organized a group to support the cause of the Five. It even included two prison officials, a captain and a lieutenant.

"René used to say, 'Principles have no price, because whoever has them won't sell them and whoever sells himself has no principles,'" said Rodolfo Rodríguez. "Their principles have helped make the Five respected in prison."

Rodolfo Rodríguez (right) in T-shirt he painted with "Free the Cuban Five" logo, together with René González (left) and another inmate at Marianna, Florida, prison.

GARCÍA: Were some of the Cubans in Marianna hostile to René?

RODRÍGUEZ: You might say they weren't so much hostile to René as they were to themselves, because they said things in his presence that could hurt, or shock. For example, someone, I don't remember who, said one day, "My mother went to Havana for cataract surgery and she had to bring her own towel and sheets."

Well, like Peter in the Bible, who marched forward sword in hand, I always spoke first. "Really," I said. "And how much did she have to pay for the operation?"

"She had to bring her own sheets. It would have been an outrage if they had charged her," he replied.

"You're right," I said. "When we took my father to the Beraja Medical Institute in Miami for cataract surgery, we didn't have to take towels or sheets. But they charged him $1,200 for each eye. I don't know how many boxes of sheets you could buy with that. Would you rather bring sheets or pay $2,400?"

Then they would tell me all kinds of nonsense.

GARCÍA: What would René do in those discussions?

RODRÍGUEZ: He'd laugh. But then he would make a comment I like a lot—and I've used it myself in conversations since then. "Look," he said, "the problem is you base your discussions on things you've heard, not on what you've seen. Look at reality, look at the entire process, follow it through to the end.

"Just think of this: How does Cuba compare with other countries? Everyone wants to compare Cuba with the North," he would say.

And it's true, you can't make such a comparison. I was in an immigration office and I saw Canadians, Australians, Chinese there—they all wanted to come to the US, because that's where all the money is that was taken from the whole world. I've never seen a rafter head south, toward Guatemala. They all want to come here. Their goal isn't to leave Cuba. It's to come here.

GARCÍA: Tell us a little about what you and René did in your idle time.

RODRÍGUEZ: There was no idle time. It bothered René when someone would say, "I'm killing time." He was never killing time. He would sit in a chair with his feet on the bed—I don't know how he could read like that—and he devoured books. I thought I was a reader. But when I saw the way he read . . . and I'm talking about tough books, too.

GARCÍA: Did you get to know René's family?

RODRÍGUEZ: Yes, it was a blessing to meet his family. I met Irma, René's mother. That woman's principles are incredible. She inspires those who meet her.

I've met all of the family except [René's wife] Olguita, although she and I corresponded a lot by e-mail when I was in prison. I still communicate with them, although I'm restricted.

GARCÍA: Let me explain to our listeners: Roddy and René, as former prisoners, aren't allowed to communicate with each under the conditions of supervised release they both face. But there's no problem with Roddy being here to talk with me and our audience.

When the family visited, did you see their love for René?

RODRÍGUEZ: Yes, and it was incredible seeing him with his daughters, Irmita and Ivette. But you've touched on something that was a key part of what I call my mental metamorphosis. It wasn't just because of the family. It was also seeing how all of Cuba supported René's cause, the cause of the Five. That had a deep impact on me.

GARCÍA: How did the guards treat René?

RODRÍGUEZ: I think everyone respected him. Except for one officer we called the "pain in the butt," but he was like that with pretty much everyone.

I'll tell you a story. I can tell it now because the person involved is no longer there. Among the prison officers there was a lieutenant, a Black man, who came to our table in the lunchroom. In front of everyone, the guard shook René's hand and said, "We support your cause." I think in private life he was a Muslim. But in uniform, in front of everyone, he came and shook René's hand.

GARCÍA: What did René tell you he wanted to do when he returned to Cuba?

RODRÍGUEZ: Well, one thing we agreed is that he and I are going to climb Mount Turquino [Cuba's highest peak]. Together with Olguita and Sandra, my wife. Sandra hasn't been to Cuba—she left when she was five and hasn't been back. But we're making plans, and she has her Cuban passport.

GARCÍA: You haven't returned to Cuba either, Roddy.

RODRÍGUEZ: Unfortunately not. But eventually I will, and when I get there I won't leave again.

GARCÍA: Did René ever seem sad or depressed?

RODRÍGUEZ: No, never. Angry, yes—on rare occasions, because he doesn't easily get mad. He said he'd never give those people the privilege of seeing him get upset or whine.

From what I've seen of their letters, I'm sure each of the Five shares that principle. There is a total fraternity among them. There is a saying that "doing is the best way of saying," and the Five truly live according to what they advocate.

GARCÍA: Were other non-Cubans interested in the issue René was involved in?

RODRÍGUEZ: Some. Many people would sit down with him and he'd talk with them.

Many inmates often came to René for help. He was always ready to translate something to English, help fill out legal forms, or get something from the library.

GARCÍA: At a certain point, before René was released on parole, you were transferred to another prison.

RODRÍGUEZ: That's right. Saying good-bye was a big moment. I have many brothers in the church—today I'm an Evangelical teacher, and soon I'll be ordained as a minister— and I love them very much, and there are many people I've learned from. But for me one of the greatest experiences in my life was getting to know René. I've said this to my family, to my wife, to my parents, who, incidentally, no longer think as they once did. They began to understand reality, because the truth is too big to hide.

GARCÍA: René is listening to this program. Do you have a message you want him to hear?

RODRÍGUEZ: I just want him to know that I'm still the same person. He's in my prayers. And I thank him for having been my friend.

In prison I saw Fernando's spirit of resistance

CARLOS ALBERTO TORRES

The following tribute to Fernando González was given by Carlos Alberto Torres, a longtime Puerto Rican independence fighter who shared five years with González at the Oxford, Wisconsin, federal prison. Torres was released on parole in July 2010 after serving thirty years of a seventy-eight-year sentence in federal prisons for "seditious conspiracy" and other frame-up charges. He was one of the longest-held political prisoners in the world.

Torres was speaking at an October 29, 2010, meeting in San Juan, Puerto Rico, organized by the Puerto Rico Committee for Solidarity with Cuba, which called for the release of all the Puerto Rican *independentista* prisoners as well as the Cuban Five. The translation is by the *Militant*.

■

GOOD EVENING, *compañeros* and *compañeras*,

In 2002, at the Oxford, Wisconsin, federal prison, as I was painting a work in oil called *Resurrection*, another inmate told me one of the five Cuban political prisoners had arrived. It was Fernando González Llort. Prison officials called him "Rubén Campa," a pseudonym Fernando had used before his arrest.

After getting to know him and a few brief conversations, he

told me his name was Fernando, not Rubén. He said, without any sign of annoyance, that the prison officials knew this but hadn't corrected it, perhaps out of bureaucratic indifference.

It seemed to me almost humorous that this Cuban, so reserved and careful, always respectful and correct, showed so little concern at being called the wrong name. I too had used a pseudonym during the years I was underground, and I remembered that after my arrest in 1980, it was actually something of a relief to be able to use my own name again.

Fernando's apparent indifference about what name he was called was a detail that revealed an important aspect of the person his experiences had created. It didn't matter to him what definition prison officials imposed, because that had nothing to do with who he was. He kept a wall between them and him. Even in these circumstances, the only thing that mattered to him was how he defined himself. He and I were in complete agreement on this.

Over time we got to know each other more and understand each other better. I learned something of the arrest of the Cuban Five. Although I wasn't familiar with the details of the charges against them and the sentences the federal court gave to Fernando, Ramón, René, Antonio, and Gerardo, it was easy to imagine the duplicity and injustice behind their imprisonment. I also didn't know, but could imagine, the abuse and isolation the five Cuban patriots had suffered since their arrest.

Before me was an honest, committed man with a deep political consciousness. Despite the hardships he had been through, he showed no bitterness over his situation. He was proud he was carrying out his duty for Cuba, his nation and homeland. I have no doubt that all five Cuban heroes, defenders of the safety of their country and their people, are men of outstanding uprightness and unbreakable commitment. The five have been punished because of the US government's hatred of the Cuban Revolution. Until I met Fernando, I thought this kind of mistreatment of prisoners was reserved solely for Puerto Rican political prisoners.

Over time we shared many things. Rare was the time that Fernando wouldn't accompany me on walks in the prison yard. They became a time to talk about everything: personal memories, heated debates, banter that sometimes tailed off into jokes or recollections of girlfriends from our youth.

During the years we were both inmates in Wisconsin, I think we got to know each other as two individuals who were fighting for their homeland and were sacrificing themselves for it as well. We reached an understanding, I believe, that the struggles for the independence of our two countries were deeply related. We are still fighting to win Puerto Rico's independence—Cuba is fighting to protect and preserve hers. There is a saying: that Cuba and Puerto Rico are petals from the same flower, sister islands with a long history of shared struggles. There, in prison in Oxford, Wisconsin, the truth of that saying was demonstrated in flesh and blood.

I learned more details about the unjust trial that kept the five Cuban heroes locked up in prison. I got to know better the character and spirit of resistance to injustice shown by Gerardo, Ramón, Antonio, René, and Fernando. And I was able to see the determination to fight and the love that marked their families.

I should say something about what the support of family members, friends, and compañeros means when you're in prison. That support is absolutely essential. It sustains us, it gives us strength when we are feeling the weight of imprisonment. The love and commitment of our loved ones helps us put things back in perspective when prison conditions get to us so much that we lose focus. It's not possible to capture

Prison officials call him Rubén Campa, a pseudonym Fernando González (**above**) used before his arrest. **Below:** Carlos Alberto Torres (in dark shirt) arrives in San Juan, Puerto Rico, July 2010, after release from thirty years in US prisons because of his activities in support of Puerto Rico's independence.

"It seemed almost humorous that this Cuban, so reserved and careful, always respectful and correct, showed so little concern at being called the wrong name," says Carlos Alberto Torres, who shared five years in Oxford, Wisconsin, prison with Fernando González. "It didn't matter how prison officials defined anything related to him. The only thing that mattered was how he defined himself."

in words the full importance of contact and visits with our loved ones.

Our jailers know this too. For prison officials, contact and visits with our families can be turned into a weapon to use against us. For the Puerto Rican political prisoners, and later for the five Cuban political prisoners as well, one tactic for attacking us has been to interfere with or deny contact or visits with our loved ones. They harass them or bar their visits. It shouldn't surprise us, then, that both in the case of Oscar and Avelino,* and in that of Gerardo, Ramón, René, Antonio, and Fernando, the tactic of interfering with family visits becomes a club to try to beat them down.

Despite the many restrictions and limitations, I had the honor and pleasure of meeting Fernando's mother and wife. They are kind human beings, tireless and dedicated workers. Not only are they doing everything they can to bring Fernando and his compañeros home. They are fighting women who defend their people with a strong sense of commitment and responsibility. Although I haven't met personally the family members of the other Cuban political prisoners, I know they too are fighting for them and support them, no matter what restrictions the jailers impose. Those same close family ties are something our patriots Oscar and Avelino have shared as well.

Today, both Cuba and Puerto Rico have patriots behind bars in US federal prisons. We have the same enemy, the same jailer. The same zombie—to use a Haitian term—who wants to bury Oscar and Avelino alive in the depths of the

---

* Oscar López has spent more than 32 years in US prisons because of his actions in support of Puerto Rico's independence from US colonial rule. Fellow independence fighter Avelino González Claudio, arrested in 2010, was released in 2013.

prison is trying to bury Fernando, Gerardo, Ramón, Antonio, and René as well.

In this battle to win our patriots' freedom—which will be like a rebirth, a resurrection for them when they return home—both peoples can support each other and fight together in solidarity until Oscar and Avelino are brought home to us and until Fernando, René, Gerardo, Ramón, and Antonio are brought back to their homes in Cuba.

"When you're in prison, the support of family, friends, and compañeros is absolutely essential. It sustains us, it gives us strength," says Carlos Alberto Torres. "In prison I got to know not only the spirit of resistance to injustice shown by the Five. I was able to see the determination to fight and the love that marked their families."

René González and relatives of the Cuban Five address 300 participants in November 2013 International Colloquium for the Freedom of the Cuban Five in Holguín, Cuba. Seated from the right, Ailí Labañino, daughter of Ramón Labañino; Irma González, daughter of René González; Yadira Pérez (speaking), niece of Gerardo Hernández; Laura Labañino, daughter of Ramón; Mirta Rodríguez, mother of Antonio Guerrero; Irma Sehwerert, mother of René; Magali Llort, mother of Fernando González; René; Olga Salanueva, wife of René; Isabel Hernández, sister of Gerardo; and (chairing) Kenia Serrano, president of Cuban Institute for Friendship with the Peoples.

How we got out of the 'hole'

RAMÓN LABAÑINO

Labañino's account was inspired by Antonio Guerrero's fifteen watercolors, "I will die the way I've lived," recording the months the Cuban Five were held in punishment cells at the Federal Detention Center in Miami after their arrest on September 12, 1998. It appeared in the Havana-based online magazine *CubaDebate*, September 11, 2013.

■

WE WERE ON THAT TWELFTH FLOOR of the Federal Detention Center in Miami for seventeen months. But it wasn't time spent idly.

From the very first days we began looking for ways to get out of our cells for recreation (one hour a day). Later we learned there was a law library prisoners could file a written request to visit using form BP-8 (also known as a "cop-out"). It was Tony who found out the library existed, and he was the first to submit a request to use it. After several rejections—and the always unpredictable attitude of the jailers (who'd pretend to be deaf, dumb, and blind, or even rip up the cop-out right in front of us)—Tony was allowed to visit it. Afterward he gave us his analysis of the charges against each of us, the possible sentences, and so forth. Then we all started going to the library.

That's how we learned you could seek a resolution of an abuse or infringement of your rights through internal prison channels, using the famous cop-outs. They go from the BP-8 form (sent to the head of a unit, in our case the "hole") to a BP-9 (to the warden), BP-10 (to the regional prison bureau), and BP-11 (to the Federal Bureau of Prisons). Once all levels have been exhausted, you can file a lawsuit against the institution. At each level there's a deadline to respond within something like fifteen days to a month.

Taking advantage of the daily recreation hour, the five of us met and decided to begin filling out the cop-outs in duplicate, with dates, requests, etc., and to record the response we received at each level. In all of these we asked to be brought into the general prison population, since there was no reason to keep us in the hole. It was a violation of our legal, constitutional, and human rights, we argued.

That's how each of us began the long road of trying to get out of the hole.

In some cases, as I said, the guards tore up the cop-outs in front of us. But since we'd made copies of everything, we'd write a detailed comment on the duplicate cop-out: "Officer Smith tore up this document in our faces, on such-and-such a date, at such-and-such an hour, in room such-and-such on the twelfth floor," and then we'd sign it. Most responses came back saying we were held there for "security reasons," and that was that.

We kept going up the levels until we reached BP-10 and BP-11. Each of us accumulated a mountain of requests with all their responses, rejections, ripped-up forms, and so forth.

Once the internal requests were exhausted, we turned everything over to the lawyers, who then filed a complaint with the judge asking that we be moved out of the hole. The complaint was accompanied by a subpoena for every guard

"After several months in 'solitary' (each of us in his cell), we were finally allowed to have each other as cellmates," wrote Gerardo Hernández. "Obviously, it was a great relief to be able to share the cell with somebody else. But after several days—twenty-three hours in the cell and one in the recreation 'cage'—we needed to find a way to pass the time. Then it occurred to us that perhaps we could make some dice."

The Cubilete Game, one of fifteen watercolors painted by Antonio Guerrero recalling the seventeen months the Five spent in the "hole" at the Miami Federal Detention Center following their September 1998 arrest.

who had ripped up our documents, every officer who had to deal with us, counselors, unit chiefs, the lieutenant in charge of the hole, even the warden himself.

On the Friday before the Monday the legal proceedings were set to begin, I recall, the five of us were in the recreation area talking. I think it was in the morning. A guard came up and asked me to come with him to speak to the lieutenant assigned to the hole.

Handcuffed, I was taken to the lieutenant. He had talked to the warden about our demand, the lieutenant said, and he wanted to know exactly what it was we wanted. The officer made clear that for "security reasons," he had no plans to move us into the general population under any circumstances.

I told him we wanted to be moved immediately to the general population, since being held in the hole was against our legal, constitutional, and human rights. That's all we were asking, and we'd continue to press our demand to the end. The security reasons were just an excuse, I argued. The "hole" was supposed to be for someone who breaks a prison rule, and the legal maximum is sixty days. What's more, we were preparing for a trial, all five of us jointly, and this situation didn't allow for adequate legal preparation.

The lieutenant responded that he wouldn't accept our request. Then there's nothing else to talk about, I said—I'd see him in court on Monday. And I got up and left.

The guards took me back to my brothers in the recreation area, and I told them what had happened. Less than five minutes later, the guard came back to take me to the lieutenant again. This time his approach was "softer." He said they had discussed the matter and had agreed to move us to the general population that day, but would place the five of us on different floors.

I didn't agree, I told him. All of us should be on the same floor, since we were preparing for a big, complex trial. We wouldn't accept anything else. If they didn't agree, we'd take it up in court next Monday.

He made a phone call and then explained it was fine—we'd all go to the seventh floor west (if I recall correctly). I wanted to take it further. I asked that we be placed two to a cell, with one of us alone.

"No, not that," he said. "Don't push me any further. Take that up with the officer in charge of the unit."

I agreed.

He said we should get ready, that they would move us shortly into the general population.

I went back to my *compañeros* and reported the discussion. We were very happy to at last be getting out of that filthy corner, the hole.

That's how it happened. In early 2000, after seventeen months, we were finally moved into the general population at FDC Miami.

Ramón is someone you're proud to know

SECUNDINO PÉREZ

Secundino Pérez came to know Ramón Labañino while they were imprisoned together at the Miami Federal Detention Center in 2009. The following account is from an article by John Studer published in the December 16, 2013, issue of the *Militant.*

■

GETTING TO KNOW CUBAN REVOLUTIONARY Ramón Labañino while in a federal prison in Miami had a big impact on Secundino Pérez.

"Ramón is a person with principles and values," said Pérez, speaking on a popular Spanish-language radio program in Miami. "He's someone you become proud to know."

Interviewed on Radio Progreso's *La tarde se mueve* (Afternoon on the Move) in January 2013, Pérez told host Edmundo García about his friendship with Labañino during a six-month period they were both in the same unit in the Federal Detention Center in late 2009 and early 2010. At that time, Labañino was awaiting a resentencing hearing in federal court. Pérez has since been released on parole.

"At first I was nervous about approaching Ramón," said Pérez, who had heard only biased propaganda about the Cuban Five from the local media, which falsely branded them

"Cuban spies." But as he got to know Labañino, "I saw the kind of person he is. We became good friends—based on respect for each other's ideas."

In conversations among prisoners, "he didn't just tell you, 'This is how things are.' He tried to get you to understand things, so you would gradually understand how things really are," said Pérez, a medical doctor who came to the US some 14 years ago from Pinar del Río province in Cuba.

In the prison world some individuals elicit "respect out of fear," Pérez said. Labañino earned a different kind of respect, one "that comes from the heart."

"He always respected everyone's ideas and beliefs," Pérez said. And everyone respected him, "even the guards."

If he saw a fellow inmate not feeling well, Labañino "was the first one to go over and try to cheer him up," Pérez said. "He didn't care what nationality you were—Cuban, Nicaraguan, whatever. He'd ask you about your problem, and if there was something he could do, he did it with pleasure. That's Ramón."

Ramón would always tell him, "Try to keep your mind occupied with something productive. Since we're here, occupy yourself with something productive like chess, read a good book, make yourself a good meal." Prisoners were allowed to buy food—fruit, vegetables, meat—and make a meal for themselves, using the microwave, Pérez explained. Ramón really liked a Caribbean dish called *mofongo*, made of plantains.

Labañino read a lot, loaned books to fellow prisoners, followed the press, and received a lot of messages of support and other correspondence, Pérez said.

"Ramón was very interested in everything that happened in Cuba, and he has a broad understanding," Pérez said. "On any question about Cuba, any issue, we would sit down and talk. He wasn't trying to convince you—we'd talk, and we would reach a certain understanding."

Pérez added, "We kept on top of the news." They listened to Radio Progreso, as well as radio broadcasts from Cuba, using small battery-powered radios. "We had to be creative. You had to stand right up against the wall" to pick up a signal.

As they discussed the US government's frame-up of the Cuban Five, Labañino showed him the trial record. "He gave it to me so I could read it, so it wouldn't be just what he said but so I could see the facts," Pérez said.

Many fellow inmates at the Federal Detention Center became convinced that the Five "had been unjustly imprisoned," he noted. By infiltrating Cuban American paramilitary groups in Florida, "they were watching out for the Cuban people, to prevent terrorism in Cuba. The trial never proved anything but that this is what they were doing."

He pointed to the selfless conduct of the Five, including separation from loved ones, not being able to tell their families what they were doing until after their arrests, and the long prison sentences imposed on them. "The things they gave up in order to protect the Cuban people—you feel indebted to them for life, because it was such a beautiful gesture full of love and sacrifice," he said.

"Ramón is a big guy"—he was affectionately known as the "Bear"—and he was an athlete in his youth, Pérez noted. But years in prison take their toll. "He's had some health problems, like with his knees, but he still exercised a lot." Labañino now suffers from arthritis, which affects his ability to walk.

Pérez said he saw Labañino's wife, Elizabeth Palmeiro, once when she came to visit at the Miami prison. "My family has met his family in Cuba and they started a friendship that has continued. Elizabeth has waged a fight from Cuba and

In prison some individuals elicit "respect out of fear," says Secundino Pérez. Ramón Labañino earned a different kind of respect, one "that comes from the heart."

Labañino (left) with fellow inmates at McCreary federal penitentiary in Kentucky, 2009. "What I learned from Ramón is that you can make mistakes in your life, but you can't live a lie," says Pérez. "When you live the truth, you have no fear. And that's Ramón."

has made efforts so his three daughters know their father is with them, in spirit even if he is not there physically. That is very important and she's done this very well and with great courage. Support from family is important for anyone who's in prison."

Labañino, along with Antonio Guerrero and Fernando González, was transferred to the Federal Detention Center in Miami in September 2009 after a federal appeals court ordered resentencing hearings for the three on the grounds that their prison terms exceeded federal guidelines. The US authorities hoped, in the words of federal prosecutor Caroline Heck Miller, to calm the "contentiousness" and "noise" stirred up by the international campaign to free the Cuban Five. At a hearing on December 8, 2009, Labañino's life sentence on trumped-up charges of "conspiracy to gather and transmit to a foreign government information relating to national defense " was reduced to 30 years.

"I remember he was feeling a little bad that evening," Pérez said. "But he's someone who bounces back, who doesn't let himself get down, and the next day he appeared more at ease. He told me, 'This fight isn't over, we have to keep on fighting.'"

Pérez said he was struck above all by the fact that Ramón "wasn't concerned about himself—he felt it was necessary to continue fighting for Gerardo."

Of the Five, Gerardo Hernández was given the harshest sentence: two concurrent life sentences plus 15 years. Although the life sentences on espionage conspiracy charges were reduced for Labañino and Guerrero, in Hernández's case it was left unchanged because the court deemed it was "irrelevant to the time he will serve in prison."

Hernández's other life sentence was for "conspiracy to commit murder," based on the false claim that Hernández bore responsibility for the Cuban government's 1996 shootdown of two hostile aircraft that had invaded Cuban airspace in disregard of repeated warnings from Havana. The planes were flown by the counterrevolutionary group Brothers to the Rescue, part of the outfit's escalating provocations designed to ignite a confrontation between Havana and Washington.

Asked how he was influenced by Labañino, Pérez replied, "I learned you can make mistakes in your life, but you can't live a lie. When you live the truth you have no fear. And that's Ramón."

When Labañino was about to be transferred out of the Miami prison, Pérez told him, "I'm getting out of prison before you, and I'll be there for whatever you need of me."

Interviewer Edmundo García was among the supporters of the Cuban Five who attended the 2009 resentencing hearings. "You saw Ramón in prison, and I saw him in the courtroom," he said in closing the program. "And there are things I will never forget."

Ramón, he told Pérez, "entered the courtroom with his hands held high, handcuffed, and turned toward the people who, as he knew, were committed to the release of the Five for the reasons you explained. He raised his handcuffed hands in a symbol of victory, and this was very moving for me."

García thanked Pérez "for this testimony of the human qualities of Ramón Labañino." These are the same human qualities that mark all the Five, he concluded, "because this is precisely the caliber of men they are."

They offered 'whatever you want' —if I would become a traitor

GERARDO HERNÁNDEZ

The following excerpt from an interview Gerardo Hernández gave filmmaker Saul Landau on April 1, 2009, appeared in the Miami-based online magazine *Progreso Semanal/Weekly*. The translation is by the *Militant*, where it was published in the June 8, 2009, issue.

■

SAUL LANDAU: Can you describe in detail what happened the day the FBI arrested you?

GERARDO HERNÁNDEZ: It was a Saturday [September 12, 1998]. I was sleeping. It was about 6:00 a.m. I lived in a small, one-room apartment. My bed was pretty close to the door because the apartment was small. I remember hearing in my sleep someone trying to force open the lock. I barely had time to react because I heard a loud sound as they knocked the door down. It was a SWAT team. They didn't even give me time to sit up in bed.

I was surrounded by people with machine guns and helmets, like you see in the movies. They arrested me, lifted me out of bed, handcuffed me, and looked in my mouth. I guess they had seen a lot of James Bond movies and thought I might have cyanide in my mouth. So, they checked to make sure that I wouldn't poison myself. I asked why I was being arrested. They said, "You know why."

They put me in a car and took me to the main headquarters of the FBI in south Florida, on 163rd Avenue in Miami. There, the interrogation began. But the arrest is the way I described.

LANDAU: They put you in the "box"?

HERNÁNDEZ: At the FBI headquarters we were each put in separate offices. They sat me in an office, handcuffed me to the wall, and interrogated me.

I had the "honor" of having Héctor Pesquera come to see me. He was the director of the FBI in south Florida, and he was Puerto Rican. My assumed identity, Manuel Viramontes, was Puerto Rican, too. I told him I was from Puerto Rico and so he started to ask me questions about Puerto Rico. All kinds of questions. Who was the governor that year? Where did I live? What bus did I take to get to school? Where did I catch it?

When he saw that I was able to answer these questions, he got really upset. He slammed his fist into the table and said, "I know you're Cuban. You're going to rot in prison, because Cuba isn't going to do anything for you."

Then, not him specifically, but the others who took part in the interrogation started to make all kinds of offers. They said, "You know how this business works. You know that you're an illegal agent. And what they say is that Cuba isn't going to admit that they sent you here with a fake passport. Cuba won't do that, so you'll rot in prison. The best thing you can do is to cooperate with us. We'll give you whatever you want. We'll change your identity, give you bank accounts."

Whatever I wanted, if I became a traitor.

"Here's the phone," they said. "Call your consulate." Strategies designed to get me to be a turncoat. This is what happened to all five of us separately. Later, they took us to the prison, the Federal Detention Center in Miami, and put us in what is called "the hole."

LANDAU: For how long?

HERNÁNDEZ: Seventeen months. The first five months were hard for the five, of course. Those of us with false identities didn't have anyone to write to, no one to write to us, nor anyone to phone. Every so often it was our turn to make a phone call. The guards would open the little window in the door, and put the phone there. "Aren't you going to call anyone? Your family in Puerto Rico?"

"No," I would say, "I'm not going to call anyone."

"But why don't you make a call?" they'd say to annoy me, because they knew I wasn't Puerto Rican and wouldn't use the phone. Those were difficult months.

LANDAU: Describe "the hole."

HERNÁNDEZ: It's an area that every prison has, for disciplining prisoners, or for protective purposes if they can't be with the rest of the population. In Miami it was a floor, the twelfth floor. The cells are for two people, but there are some people there by themselves.

For the first six months, we were alone, each in an individual cell—with no contact. Later, our lawyers took legal measures so that we could meet in pairs. But the first six months we were in "solitary confinement," with a shower inside the cell so you can bathe whenever you want. But that way you get everything in the cell wet when you take a shower.

You're in the cell twenty-three hours a day. And there's one hour a day of recreation when they take you out to another place. In Miami, it was basically just another cell, but a little bigger, with a grate that let you see a little piece of the sky. You could tell if it was day or night and fresh air would come through. That was what they called "recreation." But often we didn't go because they'd take too long, handcuffing you, searching you, your cell, taking you and bringing you back. Sometimes, they'd put us all together in the same cell and we could talk.

The regimen was very strict. It's used to discipline prisoners, as punishment for having committed a serious infraction. We were inside those four quite small walls twenty-three, sometimes twenty-four, hours a day, with nothing to do. It's very difficult from the human point of view. And many people couldn't take it. You would see them lose their minds, screaming.

LANDAU: Had you done something bad?

HERNÁNDEZ: No, we were sent there from the beginning. They told us it was to protect us from the general population. But in my opinion, it had to do with their attempt to get us to change "sides" and become traitors.

After fear and intimidation didn't work they thought, "Well let's put them in solitary for a few months and see if they change their minds."

The only thing to read was the Bible, and you had to submit a written request to the chaplain. I made the request. To have something to read, I asked for a Bible.

When they brought it to me—I don't know if it was a big coincidence or what—it had some cards inside, including ones with the telephone numbers of the FBI. Just in case I had forgotten, right? As if, "Well, this communist guy is asking for the Bible . . . he must be about to turn." I imagine that's what was going through their minds, given their way of thinking, their prejudices.

Salute to Nelson Mandela

GERARDO HERNÁNDEZ

The message below was written by Gerardo Hernández on learning of the death of Nelson Mandela, leader of the revolutionary struggle that brought down the white-supremacist regime in South Africa.

In February 1990, after keeping Mandela behind bars for more than twenty-seven years, the crumbling apartheid regime was forced to release him.

In June of that year—still on Washington's "terrorist list" (until 2008, in fact)— he visited eight US cities on a twelve-day tour. In Miami, city officials refused to welcome Mandela, denouncing him for his solidarity with Cuba and the Cuban Revolution.

■

THOSE WHO DEVOTE unlimited resources to erase and rewrite the history of Nelson Mandela, and who had him on their list of "dangerous terrorists," today will suffer from collective amnesia.

Those in the city of Miami who insulted him by denying him homage because he embraced Fidel and thanked Cuba for its aid to Africa, today will have to sit in embarrassed silence.

The Cuban Five will continue facing every day our unjust

"I was in prison when I first heard of the massive assistance Cuban internationalist forces provided to the people of Angola, on a scale one hesitated to believe," said Nelson Mandela. "For the Cuban people internationalism is not merely a word but something we have seen practiced to the benefit of large sectors of humankind."

Above: Mandela and Fidel Castro in Matanzas, Cuba, where they spoke to tens of thousands on July 26, 1991. Mandela thanked the Cuban people for their contribution to the liberation struggle in southern Africa. Gerardo Hernández, René González, and Fernando González each served as a volunteer combatant in Angola.

imprisonment, until the end, inspired by his example of unwavering loyalty and resistance.

Eternal glory to the great Nelson Mandela!

Victorville federal prison, California
December 5, 2013

The torture of Campos

GERARDO HERNÁNDEZ

The following recollection of their days in the hole was prompted by Antonio Guerrero's fifteen watercolors, "I will die the way I've lived," recalling the months the Cuban Five were held in punishment cells at the Federal Detention Center in Miami after their arrest on September 12, 1998. It appeared in the Havana-based online magazine *CubaDebate*, September 11, 2013.

■

THE ONLY THING we knew about him was his last name, which was not Campos, but I'd rather not reveal his real one.

Although he didn't talk much, he said he was Cuban and had arrived through the Mariel boatlift in 1980. The first time we saw him was when he was put in a cell facing ours in the "hole." His appearance indicated there was something wrong with him, but we didn't realize he had serious mental problems until he asked us for a magazine. We threw the line under our door to slide it under his, with the magazine tied at the end. As soon as Campos picked it up, right there, standing by his cell door, he began to tear out the pages and eat them.

We could hardly believe what we had just seen, but that same night it became apparent that his insanity wasn't faked. Sharp noises, like hammer blows, kept us from sleeping.

Those who already knew him yelled from their cells:
"Campos, please!"

The cursing got sharper as the desperation grew. Later we
discovered the source of the deafening noise: Campos—who,
of course, was always kept in a cell by himself—would lie
in the bottom bunk and kick the metal plate of the top bunk
over and over.

It reminded me of when as a child I used to make noise
banging the lids of old cracker tins, except that the racket
from Campos's bed reverberated through that entire wing of
the twelfth floor. Night after night, it became psychological
torture. Sometimes it seemed that the noise was about to stop,
that Campos had gotten tired, that we would finally be able
to sleep—but then, all of the sudden, he'd start up again and
continue into the wee hours.

During the day you would hardly know he was there—that
was when he slept. When we realized that, some of us tried to
make noise by periodically kicking the steel doors of the cells,
thinking that if we kept him awake maybe he'd sleep at night.
(That's how desperate we were!) But it was no use. Nothing
made Campos change his nocturnal habits.

We never found out whether he actually took the pills they
gave him. Maybe it was the medication that would put him
to sleep for several hours. More than once, the few times we
saw him awake during the day, he meticulously covered
with excrement the walls of his cell, the door, and the narrow window in the door through which the guards would
check on you. Unable to look inside, the guards would call
in the riot squad—the Ninja Turtles, as some called them because of their gear—who would open the door and remove
Campos by force.

As Campos's torture over several nights in a row became
unbearable, some prisoners would complain, including in

writing, until he was moved to the opposite wing of the twelfth floor. After several days of suffering, when the complaints started up again, the guards would move him from there. They'd rotate him back and forth between the two wings (east and west). That was the solution the jailers came up with to share the torture among all of us.

Campos was the first Cuban we met in prison who suffered from a mental illness and obviously needed better treatment. Sadly, he would not be the last.

From the hole

ANTONIO GUERRERO

On October 13, 2009, following an appeals court order, Antonio Guerrero's sentence of life in prison without parole was reduced to 21 years and 10 months. While waiting for his resentencing hearing, he was again held in the Miami Federal Detention Center, where the Five had been imprisoned for more than three years following their arrest in September 1998. That is where he wrote this poem.

I

Miami is before my eyes. I can't sleep.
An obstinate verse bounces
between the gleam of a skyscraper
and the tragedy of the broken shower.

Through the window I see the rising sun
glitter through the refracting panes,
in every direction people walking
with whom I make an imaginary world.

The Royal Caribbean cruise ships,
the McDonald's, the school, the banks

the homeless man rummaging through the trash
the vendor under her umbrella
are all still there and again I look at them from the
    "hole,"
that is, "from my altitude."

II

They call it Miami's Downtown,
a mass of steel, concrete, and glass
During the day a veritable ant's nest.
At night a sullen, empty place.

Ever-higher buildings,
symbols of power and opulence:
banks with transactions in the billions,
houses with few tenants.

In the cosmetic urban design
there are parking lots for countless cars.
and I don't know how to say it in verse
but what most catches my attention
is seeing that public transportation
is used primarily by Blacks.

III

Once again orange jumper.
Once again solitude among bricks.
Once again broken mattress with no pillow.
Once again shouting in the passageway.

Once again a weekly change of clothes.
Once again a tiny yellow pencil.
Once again by a miracle: a phone call.
Once again walking aimlessly.

Once again a cage for "recreation."
This time they don't even give coffee. ·
Once again dirty floor, cold shower . . .
Once again a "cop-out" for complaints,
and, of course, once again they don't respond.
Once again "hole" and once again "poetry."

"They call it Miami's Downtown/a mass of steel, concrete, and glass."

The Second Hole by Antonio Guerrero, portraying the Federal Detention Center, the courthouse, and surrounding area. "In the middle you see a little room, with a door painted black," he wrote. "That's where our 'evidence' was kept. You could count on the fingers of one hand the times we were there, each with his lawyer."

In US prison system, just going to trial earns you respect

RENÉ GONZÁLEZ

Escambray, a weekly newspaper in Sancti Spíritus province, interviewed René González for its June 15, 2013 issue, shortly after he returned to Cuba. In the excerpt below González talks about his arrest and time in prison. Translation is by the *Militant.*

■

ESCAMBRAY: How did your September 12, 1998, arrest take place?

RENÉ GONZÁLEZ: In the United States, "arrest" is a euphemism for assault. They storm your home in a show of force to paralyze you; that's the first step to try to soften you up. The federal police started beating on the door; in other cases they used a battering ram. We lived down a very narrow hall and the door was made of iron. It seems they couldn't physically knock it down. They banged on it violently and when I opened, they entered with pistols drawn. They shoved it open, threw me to the floor as they threatened me with the pistol, and immediately cuffed me.

When Olguita came out of the bedroom they threw her against the wall. Then they stood me up, asked me if I was René González, if I belonged to Brothers to the Rescue. That Saturday they took me away to prison.

ESCAMBRAY: How would you describe the first days in prison?

GONZÁLEZ: The first days are terrible. Besides, our case was different from the common practice in which they take you to a receiving area, give you clothing, explain how the prison works and let you make a phone call.

We were given special treatment; in military terms they call it "shock and awe"—they violently arrest you and take you to the FBI to see whether or not you're the kind of person who will plead guilty, who will cooperate. They immediately put you in the "hole," alone, to make you start thinking about what lies ahead for you. Those are days when you can't sleep; they didn't even give us a sheet, nothing.

At that moment the die is cast. If you didn't decide to capitulate then, you weren't going to do it later. From that point on we decided we were not going to give in, and that was that. That's what I had to confront.

Those were difficult days, right up to Monday. It was all well-staged. They keep you alone with your thoughts on Saturday and Sunday, without shaving or brushing your teeth. On Monday they dress you up like a clown and take you down to the courtroom. They make you walk down an aisle and there's this mob of people, full of hatred, looking at you shackled, unkempt, with a cadaverous look, and at the same time you're worrying about your family.

I was lucky. When they brought me out of the elevator and made me face that room full of people, and I was looking for my family, I suddenly heard a shout: "Daddy!!!" I looked around and saw Irmita giving me a big thumbs-up. From that moment on I took a deep breath and told myself: this breath will last me until this is over, and it's still with me.

ESCAMBRAY: What did you hold onto, to keep from selling out, as some other members of the Cuban network did?

GONZÁLEZ: Basically, human dignity; I believe in the value of dignity. The trial showed there are some who don't believe in it, but human values do exist. We all assert them, but under conditions like those, you see who believes in them and who doesn't. The Five believed in them. If human values exist, I don't see why a human being must give in to brute force—political convictions aside.

Just because these people have the power to mistreat me, to lock me up, I'm going to give in? No one taught me there is any value to that. In addition, there's the mission you were carrying out, the understanding of your cause, your awareness of what you were doing—knowing you are right, knowing you were defending human lives, knowing you are being tried unjustly.

All this adds up. And on top of that is the way they act. You see them lying to the judge, blackmailing witnesses, deceiving the court, defying the judge's orders, lying to the jury, coaching people to lie. As you see the depths to which they will go, you say: just how low can they get? At that point you tell yourself: I can't give in to these people.

ESCAMBRAY: You were locked up in Pennsylvania, South Carolina and Florida. How do you win respect in such a hostile environment?

GONZÁLEZ: In the case of the US prison system, just going to trial earns you a lot of respect—almost no one goes to trial. People are afraid to go to trial; the system is rigged in such a way that in a trial you will lose. Your lawyers will talk you out of it and persuade you to cooperate with the prosecutor, and cooperating always ends up meaning you have to finger somebody. What's involved? When you went to trial, you stood up to the government.

People respect you a lot for that. Besides, they know you won't finger them.

"In the US prison system just going to trial earns you respect," René González explains. **"Almost no one goes to trial. People are afraid to. The system is rigged in such a way that you will lose. Your lawyers persuade you to cooperate, and that always ends up meaning you have to finger somebody. When we went to trial, we stood up to the government. People respect you for that. Besides, they know you won't finger them."**

González talks with reporters outside US Interests Section in Havana, May 6, 2013, after renouncing his United States citizenship, a US court-imposed condition allowing him to return to Cuba.

Your attitude is important, too. If you treat people well, they generally treat you well. You must associate with people who have positive and constructive attitudes; avoid things like gambling and getting into debt; don't get involved with gangs.

The letters help a lot. People notice you get a lot of letters from different countries, and they come and ask you for stamps. The Cuban postage stamps that were issued helped. They would say: "Daaamn! This guy is on a stamp!" Even the guards asked me to autograph them on the sly.

ESCAMBRAY: Were there any cellmates or fellow prisoners in general who made an impression on you?

GONZÁLEZ: I had many cellmates. I remember one rapper who was with me in Marianna who became so involved in the case that one day he got a T-shirt and, together with Roddy [Rodolfo Rodríguez], painted the symbol of the Five on it. They went out to the prison yard and he sang a rap for the Five; they almost caused a disturbance.

Roddy is an interesting case: a Cuban with a criminal record going back to when he was a youth, including some violent incidents. When we met—although he was already in the process of changing his thinking—he had a lot of resentment against Cuba. As a result of our relationship he began to change his views about Cuba, about the revolution, about Fidel. He ended up becoming more communist than me. Sometimes I would laugh—"hey brother, give people a break, you can't argue with everybody."[*]

There was a white supermax [super-maximum-security prison] inmate who also had had a very violent past, a very dysfunctional childhood, who had ended up becoming a skinhead and robbing banks. Little by little he had been rethinking things, and as luck would have it, he shared my cell when

_____

[*] See the interview with Rodolfo Rodríguez, pp. 17–25.

he was going through this process. He approached me, we discussed a lot, and he ended up becoming politicized. Generally there's a lot of respect for us from all the prisoners.

ESCAMBRAY: Your wife Olga [Salanueva] became the pillar of the family, mother and father at the same time. However, you never stopped being the one who made the decisions in the family.

GONZÁLEZ: Come on! Olguita was the one who made the decisions in the family. I don't like directing people from afar. I trusted Olguita; my role was to do my job well where I was. I always thought it was important for them to know that I was OK, just as for me it was very important to know they were doing well.

Olguita knew what she had to do, and she did it well. Within that context, my exchanges with the girls, giving advice . . . They have always had a very open relationship with me. I'm not a cranky father. I think I'm a good father, a good friend.

ESCAMBRAY: What did you do to avoid the depression that affects every human being, especially when incarcerated?

GONZÁLEZ: That didn't happen to me. I coined a phrase that people used to laugh about. In the morning when they asked me, "How are you?" I'd say, "I'm always OK." So people would approach me and say, "I know you're OK."

I don't know; you have to fight to avoid those things. There are days when you wake up more anxious, you do get anxious. There is a certain level of anxiety, and you have to learn to recognize it and tell yourself: relax. There are days when you get up and perhaps you're a bit more irritable. That's when you have to tell yourself: don't go looking for problems.

I took refuge in physical exercise, in reading, in studying. For me it was important not to look at the time. Time won't kill me, I would say to myself, and it worked. I never ended up depressed.

I'll never allow them the pleasure of destroying our family

ELIZABETH PALMEIRO

The following interview with Elizabeth Palmeiro, whose husband is Ramón Labañino, took place in Havana on December 5, 2012.

In the 2000–2001 frame-up trial in Miami, Labañino was charged with acting as an unregistered agent of a foreign government and with "conspiracy to gather and transmit to a foreign government information relating to national defense," that is, conspiracy to engage in espionage. He was given a life sentence plus eighteen years.

In 2008 an appeals court ruled that, since there was no evidence any espionage ever occurred and no top secret information was gathered or transmitted, Labañino's sentence exceeded federal guidelines. The following year his sentence was reduced to thirty years. Were he to serve his entire term, he would not be released until October 2024.

Before the sentence was reduced, Labañino spent years in maximum-security US penitentiaries in Beaumont, Texas, and McCreary County, Kentucky. At the time of this interview, he was being held at the medium-security Federal Correctional Institution in Jesup, Georgia. He is currently at the low-security federal prison in Ashland, Kentucky.

The interview was conducted by Mary-Alice Waters, Róger Calero, and Martín Koppel.

■

MARY-ALICE WATERS: Elizabeth, to begin with, tell us about yourself. How did you and Ramón meet?

ELIZABETH PALMEIRO: We met the way most Cuban couples meet, it seems—while waiting for the bus. We kept seeing each other at the same bus stop and after a few weeks went on a date.

That was in 1989. I was working for the Ministry of the Interior as an English translator—and that's what I'm still doing.

Ramón was working as an economist in the Ministry of Foreign Trade. He had graduated from the University of Havana, where he'd been a leader of the FEU [Federation of University Students]. He also became very good at karate, winning medals in the annual university games.

We got married June 2, 1990.

WATERS: That's when all of Cuba's trade and other relations with Eastern Europe and the Soviet Union were collapsing—overnight—and what Cubans know as the Special Period was just beginning.

PALMEIRO: Yes, the economic situation was starting to get very difficult. When we went to buy household goods with the special bonus all newlyweds were given, there was almost nothing in the stores—the only kitchen utensil we could find was a frying pan!

WATERS: And Ramón began his internationalist mission in the United States two years later, in 1992?

PALMEIRO: Yes. But what Ramón told me was that he was working in Spain. He said he had a job as an economist at a Spanish company helping to get medical supplies to ease the effects of the US economic blockade. I could understand why that was important.

I didn't hear from him for long stretches at a time. Mail between Spain and Cuba was slow, and Ramón didn't call. There'd be a letter every three or four months. He wasn't here when Laura was born in 1992—he saw her for the first time when she was a year old. When Lizbeth was born in 1997, he didn't get here in time for the delivery. He arrived later that night and was home for a month.

Then he was gone again for a year and a half.

Ramón's mother didn't understand what was happening. And members of my family, as well as some female friends at work, made comments that certainly didn't help.

WATERS: Your friends were telling you to dump him? That he must be living with another woman?

PALMEIRO: Well, that was a question. But something deep inside told me Ramón couldn't be doing that, that he couldn't be involved in anything that would make me feel ashamed.

When Ramón came to visit, he'd adjust to the blackouts and scarcities here. It wasn't possible to put a good dinner on the table, but he ate whatever was served. He never complained. There was almost no transportation due to the lack of fuel, so you had to get around on a bicycle. He rode one like everyone else. He had to walk a lot. He'd lose a lot of weight while he was here, twenty pounds or so.

I never imagined that when he came home he was also going through a decompression process, because of the strain he was under.

On Ramón's second visit, in 1995, I asked for more explanation. He hinted to me that he wasn't on the other side of the Atlantic, that he was in the United States. But he still said he was working to help buffer the effects of the US blockade, trying to get access to medicine and machinery for Cuba.

My first thought was, "You're not carrying out undercover work, are you?" Because Cuba has been a victim of terrorism since 1959, and Cubans know there've been men like the Five throughout the history of the revolution, infiltrating those groups to learn about their plans.

"No, not me," Ramón said. "That would be an honor. But I am doing things that are important." He didn't even tell me he was in Miami. "Don't worry," he said. "I'm in Washington, far away from them"—far away from the counterrevolutionaries, that is.

So I calmed down. And from then on I became his rearguard. I tried to make his life easier. No more complaints. No more nagging doubts.

In September 1998 Ramón was supposed to return home. He'd just been here two months earlier when his mother died, Nereida Salazar. I cleaned the house and got ready for his return. Then I received the news he'd been arrested.

"Could this be a mistake?" I asked myself at first. "Could it be someone else?" Because the man who was arrested was named Luis Medina. Ramón hadn't told me about his double identity, of course. But when I saw the photos in the *Miami Herald*, I knew.

That's when Cuba's authorities told me Ramón's real mission: he was infiltrating terrorist groups in Florida to get information in order to avoid more deaths. After he gets out, of course, I'll find out more about what he was doing. But all five of them were involved in that work—keeping track of Orlando Bosch, Brothers to the Rescue, Alpha 66, all those terrorist outfits.

When I finally saw Ramón again in Miami in 2001, I thanked him for keeping me in the dark about his mission, for protecting me from knowing what he was doing. That knowledge would have put tremendous pressure on me, in a situation where I was taking responsibility all by myself for the family we had formed together. The day I found out, I felt deep pain. But I felt proud at the same time. It was as if a new Ramón had been born. He grew in stature before my eyes. After the arrests, the Five were put in the "hole." That's the special section of the prison where inmates are kept in punishment cells, isolated from the general population. They were kept there seventeen months, until January 2000. Even after that, I still had no communication with Ramón for another ten months, until the trial started at the end of November. Because until then he continued to go by the name "Luis Medina," who was supposedly Puerto Rican and had nothing to do with Cuba. He had no contact with his family or with the Cuban Interests Section in Washington.

I knew Ramón was OK only because Roberto, René's brother, visited René, who would say how the other four were doing. René, like Antonio, was a US citizen and didn't have to use a false identity.

So we went twenty-seven months without contact with Ramón. The same happened with Gerardo's and Fernando's families.

For that whole time, even though my parents knew Ramón was in prison, I couldn't tell anyone else—not the neighbors, not even his family. During those twenty-seven months, no one knew how tough it was, why I was so sad.

Finally, on the first or second of January 2001, after the trial began and the Five acknowledged their identities, Ramón called Cuba and spoke with me and the girls. What a tremendous joy! It was as if we'd just talked the week before.

WATERS: During the time they were in the hole in the Federal Detention Center in Miami, did Ramón have any contact with the other four?

PALMEIRO: For the first six months, each of the five was held alone in his own cell. Then prison officials began pairing them up—two by two, with one by himself. But they were still isolated in the so-called special housing unit, the punishment cells. They carried out a fight to get out of the hole, with help from their lawyers. Finally, after seventeen months, they were moved into the general prison population.*

WATERS: Were you there for any part of the trial?

PALMEIRO: No. I followed what was going on through the press from Miami. And from René's journal, since René wrote every day to his wife, Olguita [Salanueva], who had been deported from the US to Cuba in November 2000. Olguita let me read the letters, so I'd know what was happening. And whenever Ramón was able to call, he'd give me an update, too.

I didn't see Ramón until December 2001, when the Five were sentenced. Even then I wasn't able to attend his sentencing, since US officials delayed my visa until that very day. I was only able to go to the sentencing of the last two, Fernando and Tony. Ramón, like the others, was no longer in the courtroom after he'd been sentenced.

KOPPEL: Since the trial, how often have you been able to visit Ramón in prison?

PALMEIRO: During the [George W.] Bush years, I went as long as two and a half years without seeing him. Under Obama the visa process has been speeded up. On average I've visited about once a year, and right now it's twice a year.

We're allowed six visits a month maximum. So I try to organize a twenty-day trip, with six visits at the end of one month and six at the beginning of the next.

Each day I stay from the beginning to the end of visiting hours, 9:00 a.m. to 3:00 p.m. But sometimes when you arrive, they're transferring a prisoner, and they won't let you in until 11:00.

Or they say there's fog, and until it has lifted nobody can visit.

---

* See Ramón's account of this fight, pp. 33–37.

Or there's a lockdown, and they turn you away when you get to the prison entrance. That's what happened several times when Ramón was in maximum-security prisons in Beaumont, Texas, and McCreary County in Kentucky, before he was resentenced. Gerardo is still locked up in a maximum-security penitentiary, Victorville in California.

On one visit Ailí, Ramón's oldest daughter, waited an entire month and finally had to go back to Cuba without ever seeing her father. Ramón spent forty-five days in lockdown at Beaumont that time. It was one of the worst and most violent prisons in the federal system. He was there six years, from 2002 to 2008.

Then they sent Ramón to McCreary prison in Kentucky. At McCreary visits were allowed on Saturdays and Sundays only. Can you imagine? To travel so far and just be allowed to visit on the two days of the weekend! Once I went to Kentucky but was able to see Ramón only four days because of a lockdown. After that I couldn't visit him again, or even say good-bye over the phone—after not having seen him for two-and-a-half years.

WATERS: It's important to talk about these things, because these conditions are known and lived by hundreds of thousands of working-class families in the United States. It's common for the authorities to send people to prisons far from where they live, making it very difficult for their families to visit.

PALMEIRO: I've shared this experience with many families who've driven very far to visit their relatives—ten, twelve hours on the highway—and then they arrive at the prison only to find there's a lockdown and they can't get in.

RÓGER CALERO: How do other prisoners view Ramón?

PALMEIRO: They see him as a different kind of person. Ramón extends solidarity to others. Prisoners respect him.

"The aim of the authorities is to break the prisoners, and to break their families," says Elizabeth Palmeiro. "When we visit Ramón, I feel we're being treated like criminals. It's as though they want to destroy us as a family. And I'm never going to allow them that pleasure."

Ramón with wife Elizabeth Palmeiro (right), and daughters (from left) Ailí, Laura, and Lizbeth during 2004 prison visit.

They know he has many friends and people supporting him outside. They see the amount of mail he gets, the amount of literature with photos of the Five, including Ramón. That makes a difference among other prisoners—and even some guards—who know the Five are respected outside prison.

I tell our friends outside Cuba: Write to the Five, but don't be disappointed if you don't get an answer. It's impossible for them to answer all the letters they get. But it's important to write if we want to protect them.

KOPPEL: I imagine some prisoners also become interested in their political ideas and work, because they know the Five are revolutionaries, defenders of the Cuban Revolution.

PALMEIRO: Something very interesting happens inside the prisons. Many are people who've committed errors in society, more serious crimes in some cases, less so in others, but none related to politics. But when these people get to know Ramón, or any of the Five, they come to respect and even admire them.

He receives lots of material—books, newspapers, articles. Some of the prisoners who know him best ask me to send them the kind of literature I send Ramón. They ask for books, for dictionaries.

One thing Ramón does is teach Spanish classes. It helps prisoners communicate with each other. Some English-speaking prisoners are studying Spanish because they're married to women who are Latin American.

CALERO: So you've been able to meet some of his fellow inmates?

PALMEIRO: Yes. At the prison in Jesup, Georgia, I met a good friend of his, a Cuban, who arranged for his family to visit when I was there so we could meet in the visitors area. This guy always reads the newspapers and magazines Ramón gets to stay informed about the case of the Five. And he asked me for books by José Martí.

There are also prisoners from other countries—Guatemala, Colombia, Mexico—who've been cellmates with Ramón and shared the literature he gets.

He has good friends among African American prisoners too. There are a lot of African Americans and Latinos in the prisons of the United States. I don't know the exact numbers, but I don't need statistics—I see the reality in the visitors hall.

WATERS: Other prisoners sometimes make requests for a Pathfinder book or for the *Militant* after learning about them through the Five.

PALMEIRO: Each prisoner is allowed only five books in the cell. When they get a sixth book, they have to give away one of the others or throw it out. So Ramón lends the book, and it begins to circulate. These are books that educate you, that enrich your knowledge. They're being read by prisoners around him.

WATERS: I remember we got a letter from Ramón after he read one of the books Pathfinder publishes, *Cuba and the Coming American Revolution* by Jack Barnes. It explains what members of the Socialist Workers Party and the Young Socialist Alliance did in the United States in 1961 at the time of the US-organized invasion of Cuba at the Bay of Pigs, which led to the Cuban victory at Playa Girón less than three days later. We were helping organize the Fair Play for Cuba Committee and all kinds of activities.

Ramón wrote us that while he'd read many books about Playa Girón, in this one he found out something he hadn't learned from "any other book on this subject." For the first time, he said, he had a feel for "the direct influence of the Cuban Revolution, its example and impact, on the people of the US, and on the education of the revolutionary left movement and the movement in solidarity with our country" at that time.

PALMEIRO: He reads a lot—on all kinds of subjects. And I e-mail him lots of articles, so he'll be up to date about solidarity activities and other things. I can't tell him everything by phone—inmates get three hundred minutes per month, and no more than fifteen minutes per call. He has to call us; we can't call him, even in case of a family emergency.

CALERO: During your visits, can you take photos with your own camera? Or do you have to buy them?

PALMEIRO: There's an inmate whose job is to take pictures of visitors who've bought a ticket. Everything in the prison has to be paid for: photos, food from the vending machine, e-mail, phone calls. And they're expensive.

WATERS: Róger knows some of these conditions firsthand, since he was imprisoned in an immigration jail in Texas in 2002.

CALERO: Yes, a lot of what you've described was the same. You couldn't take a photo, you had to buy it. But the attitude of the prisoners was: we're not going to let them humiliate us this way. So when they got their pictures taken, they were all smiling, next to their loved ones.

PALMEIRO: It's a way to get back at them a little. Because the aim of the authorities is to break the prisoners, and to break their families. When we visit Ramón, I feel we're being treated like criminals. It's as though they want to destroy us as a family. And I'm never going to allow them that pleasure.

KOPPEL: Your preparation as a revolutionary working in the Ministry of the Interior must have helped you confront this situation.

PALMEIRO: For sure. But above all it was my education as a Cuban. Cubans understand the need for people like the Five to defend the revolution. We have a long tradition of struggle, a struggle that had to be redoubled after the revolution triumphed in 1959.

I learned that before I met Ramón. I learned it from my father, who was in the Revolutionary Armed Forces—he's now a retired lieutenant colonel. My mother says my father didn't even see me until two weeks after I was born in 1965. His military unit was stationed elsewhere. He was always away on different missions and assignments.

My father turned nineteen on April 16, 1961, the day the invasion at Playa Girón [the Bay of Pigs] began. He served in an antiaircraft unit there. He was one of the teenagers—the *niños héroes* [boy heroes], as they're known—who went to defend Playa Girón.

WATERS: We know this is a long political struggle, because the US government is seeking to punish the Five and the Cuban people for defending their revolution, for setting an example in the world. But today there are more possibilities than ever in the United States to broaden support for the fight to free the Five. Millions of workers have had experiences— like the ones you've described—with the class "justice" of the US cops, courts, and prisons. They can identify with the Five.

PALMEIRO: It's important to see the Five as normal human beings.

WATERS: And as the revolutionaries they continue to be, wherever they find themselves.

PALMEIRO: Yes, they're not languishing in their cells seeking pity. There are those who present their cases as a tragedy, a tragedy deserving of support. But we're not looking for pity. Solidarity, yes; pity, no.

For the five of them, the fact that they're in prison is part of a mission. They don't like to dwell on the health problems they've inevitably developed after being locked up for so long.

They maintain their dignity. But they haven't received the health care they need all these years. That's the truth.

KOPPEL: Like Ramón said, "I am going to wear my prisoner's uniform with the same pride a soldier wears his."

PALMEIRO: That's what he said in the courtroom, right before he was sentenced. For Ramón and for all of the Five, the prison uniform is a symbol that what they were doing was right.

WATERS: In an interview with a Cuban journalist a few years ago, Ramón said his mother had always wanted him to wear a Cuban military uniform. Yet "I was never able to tell my mother that from an early age I was in fact fulfilling her dreams," he said. "I was a *militar del silencio*—a military man in silence, without a uniform."

PALMEIRO: I prefer *"soldado del silencio,"* a soldier in silence. It captures better Ramón's discipline, his commitment.

When the people of the United States find out the truth about this case—when they see who these men really are, what they were doing, and why they were doing it—they will demand the release of the Five and support their cause. I'm convinced of that.

They will be proud to have men like these among them.

Why do we fight for the Five? Because we are fighting for ourselves

RAFAEL CANCEL MIRANDA

Rafael Cancel Miranda, a revolutionary leader of the struggle for Puerto Rico's independence for more than six decades, was the keynote speaker at a September 14, 2012, meeting in Washington, DC, demanding that the US government free the Cuban Five. The meeting marked the beginning of the fifteenth year of their imprisonment.

Cancel Miranda and four other Puerto Rican independence fighters, supporters of the Nationalist Party led by Pedro Albizu Campos, spent more than a quarter century in US prisons for their pro-independence actions. The translation of his remarks is by the *Militant*.

■

THANK YOU VERY MUCH for being here.

Why do we fight for the five? Because we are fighting for ourselves. We're not doing them a favor. We're doing *ourselves* a favor because we are fighting for us, for our freedom.

Why are the five in prison? For protecting their country. For preventing those killers from murdering their people.

You know, I've been called a terrorist. In fact, today they threatened me here in Washington. One of those rightists wrote, "A terrorist Puerto Rican is in town." That doesn't bother me. If they call me a terrorist, it means I'm doing something right. If they pat me on the back, then I'm doing something wrong. [Applause]

Now, I was in the same prison with Orlando Bosch before he set off the bomb on the plane. We were both in the Marion penitentiary.[1]

When they first brought him to Marion, the warden called me in, saying he wanted to talk to me about something. I normally didn't talk much with the prison officials. I was taken to his office and he told me, "We're going to bring two prisoners here. If anything happens to them, you're responsible." I told the warden, "As long as they don't step on my toes, everything will be all right." I didn't even know who they were, nor did the warden tell me.

About a week or two later I saw them. They were Orlando Bosch and Rolando Masferrer.[2] Every time these guys came in my direction, if I went this way they would go another way. See how brave Bosch was? Outside prison he would plant bombs in the middle of the night. But man to man, he was a coward. He would never come close to me.

1.   CIA-trained counterrevolutionary Orlando Bosch was serving a ten-year sentence in the Marion, Illinois, federal prison for a 1968 bazooka attack on a Polish freighter in the Miami harbor. Freed on parole, he went to Venezuela, where he and Luis Posada Carriles organized the 1976 bombing of a Cuban airliner over Barbados. Speaking at the September 14 meeting in Washington, José Pertierra, an attorney for the Venezuelan government in its efforts to extradite Posada, had told the story of the bombing.

2.   Rolando Masferrer was the head of a pro-government death squad in the 1950s during the US-backed Batista dictatorship in Cuba. Living in Miami after the 1959 revolutionary victory, he was convicted and jailed in 1968 on charges of violating the US Neutrality Act. In 1975 he was blown up by a car bomb, presumably by rival counterrevolutionaries.

"Thanks to Antonio, to Fernando, to René, to Gerardo, to Ramón, many millions of people have been enlightened about who the enemy is," said Rafael Cancel Miranda. **"Today it is we who thank them for the example they are giving us."**

Above: Rafael Cancel Miranda calls for freedom of Cuban Five at September 2012 meeting in Washington, DC.

Below: Cancel Miranda (left) teaching Spanish class at Marion, Illinois, federal penitentiary in 1975. Between 1977 and 1979 he and four other Puerto Rican independence fighters won their release after more than 25 years in prison.

By the way, after Rolando Masferrer got out, he was killed. They had planted a bomb in his car—they would kill each other too, you know.

We have to keep alive the names of the five. For two reasons.

First, because as we fight for them—and it is a *fight*, we're fighting for their freedom—they are giving off their light and their strength while in prison.

Thanks to them—to Antonio, to Fernando, to René, to Gerardo, to Ramón—many thousands or millions of people have been enlightened about the truth of who the enemy is.

A little while ago I talked with Gerardo by phone. It was the first time we had talked. He didn't say a single word like, "Oh, poor me," nothing like that. Men and women like him are strong.

But there is another reason why we must fight for the five. I once told [then Cuban National Assembly president] Ricardo Alarcón that we need to keep the struggle alive because we are protecting their lives. The more people get involved in fighting for them, the more careful their jailers will be about how they handle them.

■

I'm here today thanks to people like you, who kept fighting and fighting and fighting. And if I'm still alive, it's thanks to people like you. Because in the prison and in Washington, they knew there were many thousands of people watching out for us. So they were more careful.

Sometimes we get a little frustrated. Sometimes we want things to happen. But things won't happen until people make them happen. We will keep pushing, pushing.

When the Five learn about meetings like this, they feel

stronger. Not that they need more strength—they are strong. But I know that when we were in prison, every time I got a letter of solidarity, it made me feel good.

By the way, I told [José] Pertierra that I was in prison for twenty-seven and a half years. The second time I spent twenty-five and a half years because of those "firecrackers" we set off in Washington in 1954.[3]

The first time they put me in prison, I was in high school in Puerto Rico. It was during the Korean War. I was eighteen. They wanted me to be part of their army.

The first time, they put me in prison for *not* shooting. And the next time they put me in prison, it was *for* shooting. It seems that it depends who you're shooting at. [*Laughter and applause*]

By the way, *they* invaded my country. They bombarded my country on May 12, 1898, killing Puerto Ricans. And on July 25, 1898, they invaded us, killing Puerto Ricans. That was done by the US Army—the same army they wanted to put me in—and the Marines.

They massacred my people in Río Piedras on October 24, 1935, under orders from Colonel Elisha Francis Riggs, the US-appointed chief of police in Puerto Rico. In Nicaragua Riggs had been involved in the assassination of the General of Free Men, Augusto César Sandino.

On March 21, 1937, they massacred my people again in Ponce, on orders from Blanton Winship. Along with Riggs,

3. In 1954 Cancel Miranda, Lolita Lebrón, Andrés Figueroa Cordero, and Irving Flores walked into the US House of Representatives in Washington, unfurled a Puerto Rican flag in the balcony, and fired pistols at the floor below, wounding five congressmen. Convicted and given prison sentences of up to eighty-one years, they joined a fifth Nationalist, Oscar Collazo, imprisoned four years earlier for an attack on the temporary residence of US President Harry Truman.

he had publicly given "shoot to kill" orders against the Nationalists.[4]

And then they expect us to throw them kisses and roses. They invaded us, but they want us to say, "Thank you. You are so nice." And they expect us to join that army to kill people in Korea and other countries who have done nothing against us.

We can be as peaceful as we want. But that doesn't mean we have to take it, to let them do whatever they want to us. We have the right to fight back. [*Applause*]

As I said, I was in high school in Puerto Rico, nearly eighteen, and they wanted to draft me into their army, to kill Korean people. But why should I? The Korean people didn't invade my country.

I knew who invaded my country. If someone invades your country, you fight *them*, right?

They say they are not terrorists. They can kill, like they do in Iraq and Afghanistan—kill children and other people by the thousands. But those are "democratic" bombs.

When *we* defend ourselves, we are called "terrorists." When Antonio defends his people, he's a "terrorist." Ramón, René,

---

4.   In 1898 the US government declared war against Spain and seized
     its colonies in Puerto Rico, the Philippines, and Guam. US troops
     also occupied Cuba, which had fought three independence wars
     against Spain since 1868. US ships bombed San Juan, Puerto Rico,
     on May 12, 1898, and US troops invaded the island at Guánica a
     few months later, on July 25. Since then Puerto Rico has remained
     under the US colonial boot.
        On October 24, 1935, four Nationalist Party supporters were
     killed by police at the University of Puerto Rico in Río Piedras. On
     March 21, 1937, police opened fire on a Nationalist rally in Ponce,
     Puerto Rico, killing twenty-one and wounding two hundred. The
     colonial governor then was General Blanton Winship, an appointee of US president Franklin Roosevelt.

Gerardo, Fernando—they are "terrorists" because they prevented terrorism from being committed against their people.
    If that's being a terrorist, Lord, make me a terrorist all of my
life. [*Applause and cheers*]
    I forgot to tell you something. Batista put me in prison,
too.[5]
    Now, if someone like Batista—or Somoza or Stroessner or
Pinochet—doesn't like you, that means you're doing something right.

■

    Now, it was an international campaign that got me here,
to be able to be with people like you—an international campaign, and Cuba. When the United States government realized that having us in prison was no good for them, then they
were willing to do an exchange of prisoners with Cuba.[6] But
it was because of people like you.
    Carter was telling the whole world, "Human rights! We're
the champions of human rights!"
    And people would say: "But you have five Nationalists in
prison. How come they've been jailed for so long?"
    You know, we could have been out of prison much earlier—

5. Rafael Cancel Miranda recounted this episode in an interview
    published in the July 21, 2006, issue of the Cuban daily *Granma*,
    headlined, "I was expelled by Batista and embraced by Fidel." The
    interview was reprinted by the *Militant* November 5, 2012.

6. Cuba's revolutionary government had offered to release four jailed
    US agents, including admitted CIA operative Lawrence Lunt, if
    Washington freed the four Nationalists still in prison. Cuba did
    so in September 1979, ten days after the Puerto Rican revolution-
    aries returned home.

four years before the exchange of prisoners. We got out of prison on September 10, 1979. Over the previous four years, the FBI kept coming to see us in prison, offering to free us if we just asked for forgiveness. Lolita Lebrón, Andrés Figueroa Cordero, Irving Flores, Oscar Collazo, and myself—all of us rejected the proposal.

You know, we were five, too—the five Nationalists—and now we have the five Cubans.

Why did they want us to apologize or to accept conditions? Because we had become a symbol of our peoples' resistance—including the resistance of the people of Nicaragua, El Salvador, Guatemala, and other countries. And they wanted to crush that symbol.

But we told them, "You're the ones who have to ask us for forgiveness. You're the ones who bombed our country, who massacred our people."

So the international pressure was strong. And that's when Fidel stepped in. When I say Fidel, I'm saying Cuba. Because if you look for a government that really represents the people, there is one—Cuba.

I was twenty-three years old when I walked up the steps of the Capitol. Today I'm eighty-two and I haven't changed the way I think about anything.

Except that today perhaps I'm a little more revolutionary—because I know the enemy better.

Today it is we who thank the Cuban Five. We thank them for the example they are giving us.

write to:

Gerardo Hernández
Reg. #58739-004
US Penitentiary
P.O. Box 3900
Adelanto, CA 92301

**Ramón Labañino
(Luis Medina)**
Reg. #58734-004
FCI Ashland
P.O. Box 6001
Ashland, KY 41105
*Note: address envelope to
"Luis Medina," but letter
inside may be addressed
to Ramón.*

Antonio Guerrero
Reg. #58741-004
APACHE A
FCI Marianna
P.O. Box 7007
Marianna, FL 32447

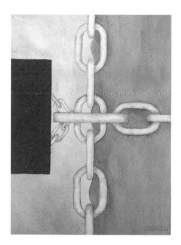

**Fernando González
(Rubén Campa)**
Reg. #58733-004
FCI Safford
P.O. Box 9000
Safford, AZ 85548
*Note: address envelope to
"Rubén Campa," but letter
inside may be addressed
to Fernando.*

FOR MORE INFORMATION

www.thecuban5.org
*International Committee
for the Freedom of the
Cuban Five*

www.freethefive.org
*National Committee
to Free the Cuban Five*

www.antiterroristas.com

The Cuban Five

New from Pathfinder!

"I will die the way I've lived"
15 watercolors by Antonio Guerrero on the 15th anniversary of the imprisonment of the Cuban Five

Fifteen paintings that graphically portray the 17 months Antonio Guerrero, Gerardo Hernández, Ramón Labañino, Fernando González, and René González spent in the "hole" at the Miami Federal Detention Center after their 1998 arrests on trumped-up charges including espionage conspiracy. The integrity, creativity, and humor displayed by the Five strike a deep chord with working people in the US and elsewhere determined to resist the system of capitalist "justice." With text by Antonio Guerrero, Gerardo Hernández, Ramón Labañino. $7. Also in Spanish and Farsi.

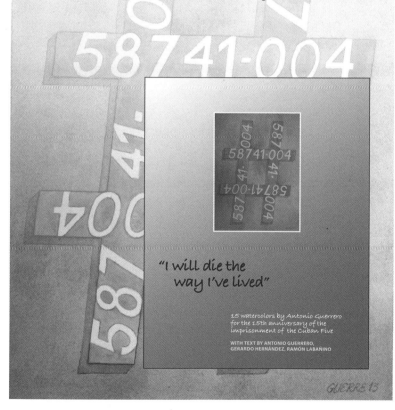

SOCIALISM ON TRIAL

Testimony at Minneapolis Sedition Trial
James P. Cannon

The revolutionary program of the working class, as presented during the 1941 trial of leaders of the Minneapolis labor movement and the Socialist Workers Party for "seditious conspiracy." Includes Cannon's answer to ultraleft critics of the defendants, drawing lessons from the working-class movement from Marx and Engels to the October Revolution and beyond. $16. Also in Spanish.

50 YEARS OF COVERT OPERATIONS IN THE US

New

Washington's political police and the American working class
Larry Seigle, Farrell Dobbs, Steve Clark

The 15-year political campaign of the Socialist Workers Party to expose decades of spying and disruption by the FBI and other federal cop agencies targeting working-class organizations and other opponents of government policies. Traces the origins of bipartisan efforts to expand presidential powers and build the "national security" state essential to maintaining capitalist rule. Includes "Imperialist War and the Working Class" by Farrell Dobbs. $10. Also in Spanish.

> "One of the ways our revolution will be judged in years to come is by how well we have solved the problems facing women."
>
> FIDEL CASTRO, 1974

Women in Cuba: The Making of a Revolution Within the Revolution

Vilma Espín
Asela de los Santos
Yolanda Ferrer
$20

Women and Revolution: The Living Example of the Cuban Revolution

Asela de los Santos
Mary-Alice Waters
$7

As working people in Cuba fought to bring down a bloody tyranny in the 1950s, the unprecedented integration of women in the ranks and leadership of the struggle was not an aberration. It was intertwined with the proletarian course of the leadership of the Cuban Revolution from the start.

Women in Cuba: The Making of a Revolution Within the Revolution is the story of that revolution and how it transformed the women and men who made it. The book was introduced at the 2012 Havana International Book Fair by a panel of speakers from Cuba and the US.

Women and Revolution: The Living Example of the Cuban Revolution contains the presentations from that event.

Both titles also in Spanish.

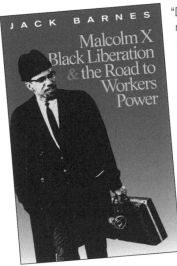

EXPAND YOUR REVOLUTIONARY LIBRARY

The Working Class and the Transformation of Learning
The Fraud of Education Reform under Capitalism
JACK BARNES

"Until society is reorganized so that education is a human activity from the time we are very young until the time we die, there will be no education worthy of working, creating humanity." $3. Also in Spanish, French, Swedish, Icelandic, Farsi, and Greek.

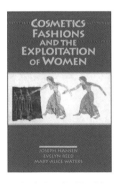

Cosmetics, Fashions and the Exploitation of Women
JOSEPH HANSEN, EVELYN REED, MARY-ALICE WATERS

Sixty years ago, an article published in the socialist weekly *The Militant* sparked a lively debate on how the cosmetics and "fashion" industries play on the economic and emotional insecurities of women and youth to rake in profits. Today that exchange, contained in this book, a Marxist classic, offers an introduction to the origin of women's oppression and the struggle for liberation. $15. Also in Spanish and Farsi.

Puerto Rico: Independence Is a Necessity
RAFAEL CANCEL MIRANDA

In two interviews, Puerto Rican independence leader Cancel Miranda—one of five Puerto Rican Nationalists imprisoned by Washington for more than 25 years until 1979—speaks out on the brutal reality of US colonial domination, the campaign to free Puerto Rican political prisoners, and the example of Cuba's socialist revolution. $6. Also in Spanish and Farsi.

WWW.PATHFINDERPRESS.COM

Titles in this series

EDITED AND INTRODUCED BY MARY-ALICE WATERS

BY ANTONIO GUERRERO (2014)

Voices from Prison: The Cuban Five
BY GERARDO HERNÁNDEZ, RAMÓN LABAÑINO,
RAFAEL CANCEL MIRANDA, AND OTHERS (2014)

Cuba and Angola: Fighting for Africa's Freedom and Our Own
BY FIDEL CASTRO, RAÚL CASTRO, NELSON MANDELA, AND OTHERS (2013)

Women and Revolution: The Living Example of the Cuban Revolution
BY ASELA DE LOS SANTOS AND MARY-ALICE WATERS (2013)

Women in Cuba: The Making of a Revolution Within the Revolution
BY VILMA ESPÍN, ASELA DE LOS SANTOS, AND YOLANDA FERRER (2012)

The Cuban Five
FROM THE PAGES OF THE 'MILITANT' (2012)

Soldier of the Cuban Revolution
BY LUIS ALFONSO ZAYAS (2011)

Capitalism and the Transformation of Africa
BY MARY-ALICE WATERS AND MARTÍN KOPPEL (2009)

The First and Second Declarations of Havana
(2007)

Our History Is Still Being Written
BY ARMANDO CHOY, GUSTAVO CHUI, AND MOISÉS SÍO WONG (2005)

Aldabonazo
BY ARMANDO HART (2004)

Marianas in Combat
BY TETÉ PUEBLA (2003)

October 1962: The 'Missile' Crisis as Seen from Cuba
BY TOMÁS DIEZ ACOSTA (2002)

From the Escambray to the Congo
BY VÍCTOR DREKE (2002)

(continued on next page)

PATHFINDER AROUND THE WORLD

Visit our website for a complete list of titles and to place orders

www.pathfinderpress.com

PATHFINDER DISTRIBUTORS

UNITED STATES
(and Caribbean, Latin America, and East Asia)
Pathfinder Books, 306 W. 37th St., 13th Floor
New York, NY 10018

CANADA
Pathfinder Books, 7107 St. Denis, Suite 204
Montreal, QC H2S 2S5

UNITED KINGDOM
(and Europe, Africa, Middle East, and South Asia)
Pathfinder Books, First Floor, 120 Bethnal Green Road
(entrance in Brick Lane), London E2 6DG

AUSTRALIA
(and Southeast Asia and the Pacific)
Pathfinder, Level 1, 3/281–287 Beamish St., Campsie, NSW 2194
Postal address: P.O. Box 164, Campsie, NSW 2194

NEW ZEALAND
Pathfinder, 188a Onehunga Mall, Onehunga, Auckland 1061
Postal address: P.O. Box 3025, Auckland 1140

Join the Pathfinder Readers Club
to get 15% discounts on all Pathfinder
titles and bigger discounts
on special offers.
Sign up at www.pathfinderpress.com
or through the distributors above.